The Genealogist:

All My Best

Friends are Dead People

N. L. Gray, PhD

*I spend too much time with dead people and my little roots grow on the inside
rather than on the outside. I rarely need watered in the present---it's the past the
comforts me, and there is only so much water you can drink...when you are dry.
And dead people are never thirsty.*

N.L. Gray

N.L. Gray

Chapters

BECOMING A GENEALOGIST
Chapter 1

Don't be offended at my calling the folks I research 'dead people'. They are dead and they were people. I like this much better than euphemisms that make genealogists seem like grave diggers.

I spend more time with dead people than I do with the living. To me, dead people are less dramatic, less confrontational and less assertive. For instance, when you find a dead person in a chart, the living will sometimes tell you that you that you are wrong—drama. And dead people never yell at you if disagree with what grandma said about the family line—confrontation. And lastly, I have never known a dead person who insists that you pick up the pace when researching their chart—assertive.

Becoming a genealogist isn't easy. You have to be curious, diligent and have the willingness to become exasperated at a moment's notice. Everyone insists they have Native American blood—but when documents that say they do not, I always hear, "But Grandma says…" Grandma can be exasperating at times, but then I love dead people, and Grandma is dead.

Sometimes it is tempting to just give them what they want, but then you can never look into a computer screen again with the same self respect. It is all about the research and being 'right'. You

always have to be right—like a pirate. Pirates never lie. Dead people never lie either. Lying is for the living. That is why very little of what your client may say is true—Grandma put them up to it.

But then there is no better feeling than to find a dead person in a tree that no one else could find. Not that your client (the living) may want you to find them. There are always drunk dead people, illegitimate dead people, prison dead people and old man and young woman (ex. 15 year-old

girl marries a 52 year-old man) who are now dead. There are millions of ways to offend your client, so be ready for the 'is to—is not' game. No matter how much documentation you have, someone will always disagree (Grandma again). If you have a particularly unbelieving person, print

everything and give it to them. You may end up killing an entire tree in the process, but you will have the living person preoccupied with reading and counting the pages.

Printing does have other purposes, however. Finding a link

you have lost with valuable information can be frustrating. I save

links to my genealogy pages by pasting them into a Word file or a text file by copying the links. That way I can run a name search on my computer and find it.

But there is information that should be printed. Archive documents should be scanned, but also should be printed. Oral histories should be scanned as well, but they should always be printed. Anything that you can't find on the internet, should be scanned and printed.

Printing has other purposes as well. Sharing documents is possible if you have printed copies and you may also want to give copies to a client.

Another purpose is just organization. Unless you have four

or five computers laying around, you can't get all the information at once—which you will need to move forward. Comparing records isn't easy on the internet.

Scanning and printing is a great way to help you organize your documentation. And you can pull something out quickly. In case of fire, you can grab your printed files or your computer, or both—

never lose documents. You most likely will never be able to find them again if you don't have copies.

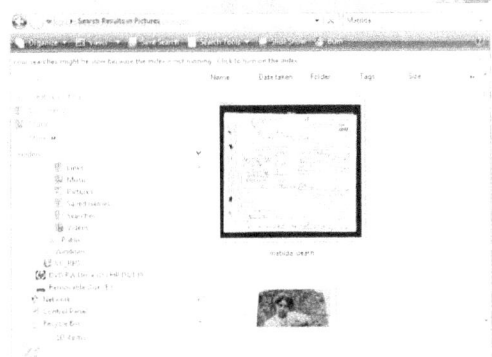

When you are saving pictures and documents make sure you name the picture or document an easily readable file name for later printing or storing. I use the name of the person I am saving—this way I will never forget who it is and I will always be able to search for it.

I have been doing genealogy for the past 25 years. I have seen it all. I started before the internet was of any use and I spent most of my time sending away for archived documents and interviewing

family members. I scanned every picture I could find or was given to me by a distant aunt or uncle— everyone wanted to be remembered. That's how I see it—I am a collector of the memories of dead people.

I have 11,663 people in my genealogy tree, and I am hoping I can stop finding branches. However, anyone who has ever been on Acestry.com knows that in one day you can easily find a 1,001 files. But every file is unique to that dead person. It says something about how that dead person lived and how old they were when they died. Most dead people, of dead people age, had infants who succumbed to various illnesses and Grandparents lived with their sons and daughters when they became old or widowed. Some things have changed a great deal since then.

Sometimes what you find can bring shame; other times it can

bring sorrow. And then there are times they bring joy. You become attached to this sorrow, suffering and joy. This may be a great aunt or a distant grandmother. As you search and learn their stories, you may see yourself in their paths, and that is when they become special to you and they make you want to dig even more.

I became attached to my paternal grandmother when she became lost in my tree. I found her living in a poorhouse abandoned by her mother and paternal and maternal grandparents, as well as her father. I have one picture of her. She looks angry and frightened, like she doesn't know how to feel any other way.

I also became attached to my maternal great great grandmother. She was from Scotland and had died in childbirth. I felt so much sorrow for her, I had to start the dig. Because she was from Scotland, I purchased the world

subscription to Ancestry.com. The only clue I had was the name pattern used in Scotland. It was a very odd name so I found her father and her great grandfather and her great great grandfather, as well as their wives. Any tiny bit of information, including the cultural norms of naming could help you find a lost relative in your tree.

Checking census records can also help, but make sure you read all of the information. I found a great great grandfather who was born at sea. They can also give you the names and the birthplace of parents and the work your less distant relatives were engaged in. I have found cherry pitters, farm laborers, shoe makers, blacksmiths and merchants. I also found that most of my relatives lived in close proximity to one another. Lost relatives can often be found living near the homes of one another or living in the same home.

Now that I have given you some background information, let's get started. Make a strong pot of coffee (if you drink coffee) lots of papers and several pens—you will need a computer (laptop or desktop) and access to the internet. Find a comfortable chair near a printer/scanner and get ready to work. It is time to

make friends with your dead people.

THE HAZARDS OF BEING A GENEALOGIST
Chapter 2

There are many hazards you need to consider, including weight gain, numb parts, sleeping parts, and obsession. Some can

be dangerous, others just annoying. All of them have an effect, however, on both your psyche and your body.

I'll talk about weight gain first. No matter what you try to do, as long as you're sitting in one spot searching for the birth certificate of your great uncle's mother-in-law, you will eat. It is like reading a text book or studying for a test, you kill the in-between times or the boredom with food.

Trying to eat healthy foods is always a plus—unless you find you've eaten seven bananas within a two hour time period. Peanuts can be deadly. As you sit munching, you forget that a pound of peanuts is unhealthy and can cause coronary disease and hypertension. Licorice,

although tasty, can put you in a sugar high. Although it may seem beneficial to be rushing through data, licorice can be the one of the

most detrimental foods for research.

Expect to gain a minimum of ten pounds over your first three months of researching. You may try pedaling a recumbent bike with your computer on your lap, but this rarely works, if ever. I would suggest eating carrots over the six straight hours you will spend in front of a screen, but that rarely works either.

Perhaps the only thing that does work is periodically moving around. Stand up and stomp your feet while you spend time at the computer. This will provide exercise and it's harder to eat when you are stomping and typing at the same time.

Now let's talk about falling asleep parts. You may find parts

falling asleep that you didn't know could fall asleep—most importantly your legs. I ended up riding in an ambulance a few weeks ago when I stood up too quickly and fell over my overflowing ottoman. I could barely walk and was using an old shovel handle to hobble around. When the ambulance driver and EMT arrived, I was quick to say I had been doing yard work, and hence, the shovel. I insisted on walking to the ambulance with my broken shovel while dragging my left leg.

I spent a full day in the ER. I was given morphine and had to lie in the hospital bed for several hours while the pain subsided. When I left, I was given a bottle of pain medication and then limped from the hospital on my broken shovel. When my daughter arrived to pick me up from the hospital she said, "Why are you limping around on a shovel". I answered that I had been doing yard work. There was no way I could tell her I fell over the ottoman. She'd had to leave work to pick me up.

It's not just your legs that will fall asleep; it's your buttocks, your ankles, your hands and your feet. Once something begins to tingle, you need to quickly find a way to wake it up. I shake what I can and lift what I cannot. Taking a break will help avoid this hazard, but after hours at the computer, it is easy not to notice when you've reached the danger point.

Also, never dangle your feet—it causes your ankles to become weakened and you lose your balance more easily when you stand up (at least that is my assessment). I am only 5' 1" and my feet never touch the floor while I am sitting. I have a Webster's

Unabridged Dictionary under my TV tray on which to prop up my

feet. This works well during long sessions at the computer. When necessary, I shake out my feet, stretch my ankles and move on to the next dead person.

Back aches are probably the most common hazard. My back hurts right now. Try to sit up straight and not slump forward. If you choose to, you can place another Webster's under your laptop to raise it up from your TV tray. This will give you a straight line of sight and minimize spine trauma.

You neck can also be affected. In this case, find a way to keep your head from tilting forward. If you wear bifocals, use them. This way you can look down without stretching your neck. If you don't wear bifocals, find a lower chair.

You can also damage your eyes by staring at the screen for

hours. If you are not careful, you will be wearing bifocals over your

bifocals. Avert your eyes occasionally; move your eyeballs back and forth, look off into the distance and have a cup of coffee.

Which brings me to my next hazard—coffee. You may find yourself drinking pots of coffee (if you drink coffee). You may also find yourself drinking soda or black tea. Whatever you decide to drink, you will be running to the restroom, twitching and still doing your best to find that 5,000[th] dead relative you have been obsessing about.

Not using the restroom can also be a hazard. Who wants to get up and run to the restroom when they have just reached the year 1640 and found they were part of some obscure revolution. But not

 using the restroom can cause all sorts of difficulties only a medical book is qualified to describe.

Remember, you can always come back to your computer. However, not everyone wants to leave their chair and other medical issues are a bit more complicated.

For instance, colds and allergies. Keep a box of tissue handy. No one wants to grab a box when they are in the middle of a 16th century search. Too many sneezes can make your screen blotchy and you may miss valuable information. Now I know that this a disgusting thought, but you will appreciate it later.

This brings me to my final hazard.Obession. I have my laptop sitting on a TV tray in front of my favorite overstuffed chair.

Several times a day, I walk past it to see if there are any more Ancestry 'leaves' to look over. My laptop is always on and the Ancestry page is always open so it isn't hard to see new sprouts. Once I see a sprout, I have to see where it leads. Sometimes, most of the time, it leads nowhere, but I can't stop myself from looking. This morning, at 2:46am, I was cultivating my sprouts because I just knew there would be some invaluable information under that leaf. There wasn't, but at least I could sleep now. If those little leaves ever get sound effects, I will be lost.

Now that you know about the hazards, you will be able to research in relative safety. Your dead people will appreciate all you are doing to make sure they hang from your tree. No one who is dead wants to be left out; and that is why there will someday be 40,000 people in my tree. Or more.

WILLING TO SHARE
Chapter 3

Philander Hiram Gray
1st Oregon Infantry Nov. 1864 - Jan 1865

A lot of people will contact you asking to share your information. It is up to you as to decided whether or not to share your information. Some people feel protective of their research and/or their family history, and that is fine. In the beginning, I think we all feel that way

I was uncomfortable sharing; mostly because I was afraid I was wrong. I started researching when computers didn't have hard-drives and I only wished I had a-hard drives. I spent a lot of time in libraries, archives, museums and newspaper offices. I collected oral histories and sent away for what might be documents when I knew where someone had lived. This was

always hit and miss. Not everyone lived where they were said to have lived. A mistake you may not want to share.

I found, however, that lots of people make mistakes. Those mistakes are passed from one researcher to another, Because those mistakes can be shared, sharing is not always beneficial.

Sometimes sharing is beneficial, however. The person who wants to share information can become an asset when you are looking to make corrections to a branch of your family tree.

You also find cousins you never knew you had and soon you have a wealth of information, including pictures and other documents. I have only found one person that I wished had never found me. Now I have made certain she will never find me again.

When you meet someone who makes your genealogical life a living hell, write down their name, mark return to sender on all of their letters, and now that the internet is available—block them. Arguing with someone serves no purpose. Someone who is demanding is a pain. I dislike pain.

Another important thing to remember is not everyone will agree with your research. They will change birthdates, places someone has been born or where they have lived, parents and how they spell their name. Who is right? You may insist you are and that may be the case, but knowing for sure can be difficult without more research. Take another look at you discoveries. You may be surprised at what you learn. But then again you may not. You may be surprised to learn what is wrong, But then you may not then, either.

For instance, I had a man email me at one point. He was doing paid research on my family tree. He contacted me to say how interesting it was that my great grandmother was from England. Well, she wasn't. I knew her. I decided not to share because he was  being paid, and if that were the case then he could research things on his own. Obviously there were gaps on his expertise. I may look him up and send him a copy of this book.

There is a lot of arguing that goes on between professional genealogists, dabblers and families. One message I got recently very strongly stated the middle name on one of my branches was "Dempsy" not "Dewey". I checked and the only middle name I had was an initial, so I was neither right nor wrong. But some people get touchy—even about initials.

 Today, in fact, I had a woman mention that I had two different census records for the same year on one on my seedlings. I let her know that often times I will add more

than one census record to help verify other family members. She said, "Good luck with your little endeavor." My endeavor is hardly little.

I now have 22,000 people in my tree (things move quickly) and I am willing to share anything I have researched. I am in the process of checking links and making sure I am correct. But

weeding begets from more obscure relatives, and more obscure relatives from begets means you really don't care if someone copies

information on the step-son of your uncle-in-law of your great grandmother's third husband (more on this later).

Weeding is a joy for me. Some days I can only hope that I will find a disconnected link as I go through my data and I get giddy

when I hit delete. The fewer non-meaningful tree members you can weed the better. Not something a beginner may understand, but you will get there. But make sure you are right, even with those dead people you have deleted. Someone will always be on the search for that one person. And that person still exists, as does the research, it is just that his or her leaf has been plucked from your tree.

If you do decide to share, make sure you don't include living relatives—they will hate you for it. Privacy is a big deal when it comes to collecting your roots and the low hanging fruit is nothing you want to pluck from your tree. I have inadvertently included someone I thought was dead, only to find they were alive. Nothing hurts worse than finding yourself dead in a chart. Nothing is more embarrassing either. So check with other relatives before you share the image of your supposed headstone with nearly a million users

As far as finding that millionth headstone that is undoubtedly not yours, someday it may be out there; but my preference is to wait. I am always willing to share as long as I am not counted as a dead bud.

But then once you start collecting buds (branches is too big a word here) there is a count and an order that starts to form , which grows into an 'where did that go'. Yet at 22,860 (time  has passed) someone may ask you to share information on number 22,822. But much of the name they give you is incorrect, the birth date is incorrect. Pretty much everything is incorrect. Where do you go from there. The truth. I don't know.

And then they are times you do know. Yet, you only have hard copies of the data. I keep my hard copy data in a recliner ottoman with a lid. Asking me to look up some relative that on my personal computer and in my ottoman can be impossible since the information is yet to be uploaded to the internet. What do you do? I kindly tell people to check back with me at a later date. They always do and I ask them to check back with me at a later date. Then they send me a notarized letter demanding the information (a bit of sarcasm there). I tell their lawyer to check back with me at a later date.

I always like to ask why someone needs the information, as well (another reason not to share the living and confine you tree to the dead). I had my identity stolen a few years back so when someone asks to include me in their tree, I just say 'no'. If you do share the names of the living, a treacherous individual will  then know your mother's maiden name and they can give it to the bank. They may also so get the information from a public obituary, but why make things easier for the thieves.

Sharing what and how is your choice. If you want to, it is a great way to get additional information. Just be selective. No one wants their toes to curl when they find the person they shared their information with is a scoundrel (this includes those who are a pain). People crawl out of the woodwork (no pun intended) nearly every day. Let them ask and politely say yes, or even more politely say no. You never know when you might need them someday.

TRANSCRIPTS
Chapter 4

Transcripts are words that come from far away voices, and they can read or heard. They come in all forms and fragments.

 They can be oral histories found in libraries and archives. They can be typed or handwritten scraps of paper found in a manila envelope, The one thing they have in common is they tell a story.

The best way to start you search is to ask. I have never met a museum curator or librarian who wasn't happy to help. They have collections that gather dust in drawers and they are more than happy to share them.

I have had the best luck finding transcripts in smaller libraries and museums. In one library in a town of about 5,000, I found stacks of transcripts of oral histories. An archivist collected several hundred pages from the oldest members of the community and then had them placed in the library. She labeled each transcripts with the name of whom she collected the history, but also names mentioned in the histories. I made copies of anyone's name that sounded even vaguely familiar.

When I read the transcripts. I found that one of the relatives I had grown attached to was a school teacher of the first school built in the center of several frontier towns. A few years later, according to library records, he had helped settle a stage stop that had more bars and 'bawdy' houses than it did churches. The sheepherders in the area came down each fall and spent time in the town. It had a rich history until the train was built along the other side of the

desert and the town became nothing but rubble. According to the transcripts, those in the area collected stone and other bits and pieces of the town as souvenirs,

as well as to make improvements to their own homes.

Although my grandmother's name wasn't mentioned at the top of the page where all the participants names were listed, I did find her swimming in a hot spring with her cousins and enjoying her time with her extended family, since she was an only child.

You really never know what you will find in transcripts and often times you have to read the fine print. But all of this information can lead to a driving trip or a family reunion where you circle the places on the trail and look for artifacts.

Much like transcripts, old phonebooks can help fill in the blanks. Finding where a dead person lived means you can see if they were from the right side or the wrong side of the tracks. If they were poor, middle class or wealthy. Homes and streets paint another picture of your dead person's past life.

Some genealogists want only to glance and store. I like to build my dead people's lives as completely as possible. I want to know where they lived and why; I want to know their friends and their enemies; I want to unbury (pun intended) their stories and bring them back o life. Dead people love being remembered.

Remember, however, to build your own transcripts before your elderly family members are gone. These transcripts are as valuable as any you will find in a library, if not more. Do this before you person becomes a dead person. The best history is from those you can hear and see as they smile and remember.

BIBLES AND LETTERS
Chapter 5

Letter may be found in old bibles or in shoe boxes. Ask family members if they have any old stories lying around and you may find unearthed gold. Much of it may seem mundane, but when you add those words to a picture and build a story, you see things you have never seen before and form a bond with your long lost dead person.

Most recently, a family member I met through a genealogy site realized she had wedding pictures of the daughter of my great great aunt, Along with the pictures were wedding invitations and letters that gave a full depiction of what life was like in the late 1800s.

Sometimes you will find the writings of would be authors. These letter often share the minutest detail of the harshest life. Bibles often include similar information. It was in a bible that I found a second cousin had been killed in a 'twister', His father had been killed as well and his mother had been paralyzed. I hadn't thought much about the devastation or horror that my Arkansas must have gone thought with no alarms or forecasts, just a darkening of clouds.

All of these stories in the bibles and letters made me want to dig for more—not just names, but people—how they lived, where they walked, whether they picked up the same stone I touched. These were all stories I found in letters and bibles.

In another bible, I found a complete genealogy list that was written in the 1880s. The list included how the people had passed, who they married and a brief history of each of those in the bible. It was written by the mother of the children all born in the 1800s. It was amazing to find such a treasure.

I believe everyone should write their own histories in a bible. Bibles are rarely lost or destroyed and the information can be as detailed or as brief as the author chooses. I don't have a bible full of names and histories, but I do have a genealogy book where I have written what would be kept in a bible. I am hoping someone cherishes it as much as I do.

A lot of people these days just use electronic methods to write their history, but there is nothing more rewarding than to find something written in the actual hand of the author. I have filled up several journals that will serve that purpose. But just remember to tear out the pages you would prefer no one ever read. And there will be a few. And they will be embarrassing. And after you tear them out, you may decide burn them. Just remember to do it before you are one of the dead people. Dead people keep no secrets—that is if they have written them down.

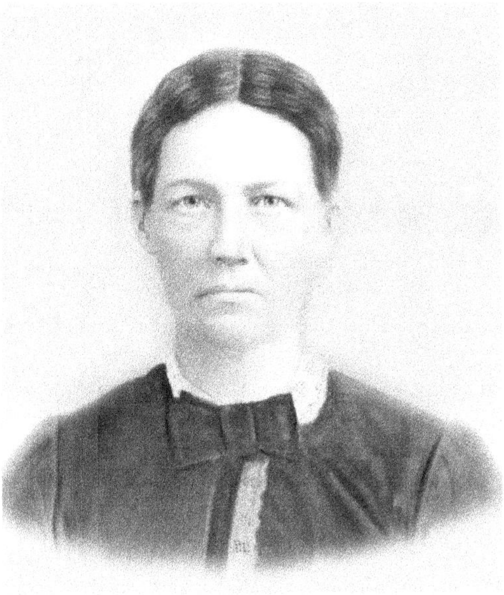

ONLINE STATE AND NATIONAL ARCHIVES AND CENSUS RECORDS
Chapter 6

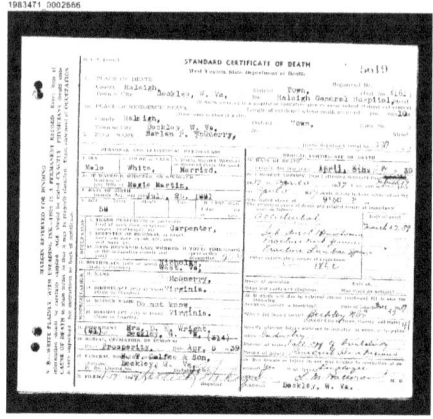

Birth. marriage. divorce death , catastrophes can all be found in state and federal archives.

Birth records are one of the most critical records you can find. If you don't find someone you know should be there (grandmothers, grandfathers, uncles, cousins), off to search again. You may have to go through 20 census records, but sooner or later you will find what you are looking for and perhaps more. In census records, realize that names may have been written phonetically. I always look at the names of family members and who might be living in the same areas. For example, one of my relatives had the last name of Alberson, that was constantly being changed to Albertson. But I found the family members by looking for other family members I recognized. Ethnic names can change even more. But keep digging.

It took me years to find my maternal grandmother, Matilda. She wasn't born illegitimate, but she was born four months after the marriage. When her mother remarried, she had Matilda placed in an orphanage that also held prisoners and the insane. It took me years to find her until I had read about the orphanage situation. When I began searching the poor houses, I found Matilda. She was listed as Ilda Adkins. Her birthrate was the same and I traced her to the marriage to my grandfather. She died at 35 from what is believed to have been a heart problem contracted after being exposed to rheumatic fever.

Looking through census records that can be found for free are a wealth of information that can surprise and bring sorrow, like with Matilda

I found it interesting that how many children who were orphans were placed as housekeepers and farm hands. If you are looking for stories and not just names, look into the archives.

Death certificates most often have the names and maiden names of the parents if you get lost somewhere on your trail to find your ancestor. They usually have the cause of death. This can be helpful if you are looking for health histories, and for myself, I did find that the males in my father's family died young from heart ailments. I have made changes to my life in consideration of this so I don't end up with my dead people.

Marriage records are also a wonderful asset. Maiden names are listed on records as well as where the couple was residing at the time of their marriage. Parent names are also included and sometimes witness names that are familiar can help you track down where the couple lived.

I keep a spreadsheet to track connections no matter how mundane they may seem. If I find even the smallest bit of information, it can usually lead me down the road to finding another dead person, the one I may have been searching for all along.

It is fairly easy to find genealogy sources these days, but I am including few places to get started. I have used them all to search for relatives, but and be sure to look for archives in your own states, since most states have archives. I would run a search on your archived sites first, but there is also RootsWeb and bulletin boards. I found four close family members using bulletin boards. Family sites are also helpful.

Be careful not to go to a paid site unless you know where you are headed. Look for .gov or .org sites or sites that are familiar like Ancestry.com. You don't want to end up paying for something you don't need.

Places to Start

http://www.wvculture.org/history/genealog.html

http://nsla.nv.gov/Archives/Nevada_State_Archives/

https://www.archives.gov/research/catalog/

https://history.idaho.gov/idaho-state-archives-genealogy

http://sos.oregon.gov/archives/Pages/records.aspx

https://familysearch.org/

https://ancestry.com/

LIBRARIES, NEWSPAPERS AND MUSEUMS
Chapter 7

Libraries and Museums have transcripts and old newspaper articles often bound books dated by year. They have microfiche, census records and photos. Copy any that seem even slightly related to your quest. You may find a treasure you wouldn't have found had you just looked for last names. I have found a great deal of

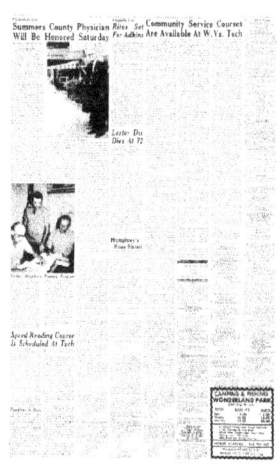

information by looking at dates and towns and legal records.

For example, while in a library, I copied every newspaper clipping of anyone I thought even may be related. When I got home I began reading, I came across an article about someone who had the same name as my great great uncle, which later I found out he was a distant relative. As I read further, I found that there was more than one article about Lafayette because he had been shot and killed while gallivanting with another man's wife. According to the articles, my great great uncle Lafayette, ran from the house in his underwear and was shot dead in the yard, The husband was never charged since Lafayette was caught with his pants down.

Another set of clippings was far more tragic. I found that another great great uncle had lost his family in a fire. There were five children and his wife. My great great uncle didn't spend a lot of time at home and he liked to visit other women and spend time in the saloons. I knew of this great great uncle before I had read the story of the fire. It was devastating to know that he had been away drinking when the fire occurred.

I found that my father, his brother and a cousin had stolen bread and other food from a school. The article said they were hungry and had no jobs. This was in deep woods of West Virginia. They were 16 and 17 years old. The judge had given them a choice—go to jail or join the military. Of course, they all three chose the military. I read similar articles with criminals being given the same choice. The boys became men, as the judge would say, and just in time for the Korean war.

I read a lot of newspaper articles—even those I didn't need to read. I always found something of interest, whether it was the cost of a pound of butter or the anniversary of two high school sweet hearts. I think curiosity is one of the most important attributes necessary to be a good genealogist. You must also want to be a historian if you really want to build a picture of your dead people.

Museums often have a treasure trove of transcripts, microfiche, original photographs of postmasters assessors, and mayors. While in a museum, I found a picture of my great great grandfather because he  had been a postmaster,. The museum also had pictures of World War I registration cards. There were pictures of the small towns that no longer existed and pictures of the long unseen landscapes,

The librarians and museum curators were wonderful. When I have shown interest in a document or photo, they have gladly pulled it from their case so I could take close-ups of the pictures. Others would make me copies of documents while I was there or mailed them to me later.

Museums and libraries also may have phonebooks. It was exciting to see where my dead people had lived and I would drive by their houses taking pictures and hoping no one inside drew a gun. Again, genealogy isn't just about names in a book. It is a history of someone who lived long ago and lives again through pictures and documents.

PHOTOGRAPHS AND POSTCARDS, PRESERVING AND REPAIRING
Chapter 8

Photographs can be a precious find especially if you are able to collect them from family members. I always scan the original and then return it to the owner. This way there is no conflict with other family members.

I also share the photographs I have collected by creating keepsake books. I have made several using software intended for the publication of books (later on this in the Creating Keepsakes chapter). Sometimes I have created CDs to distribute at family reunions and of course funerals. May seem tacky, but it is the one place that everyone is usually present.

When working with pictures, on Ancestry or through other methods, make sure you check the information. If others have the same pictures from another source with other names, you will need to do more research. Usually this means tracking down someone who knew the individuals in the pictures—and this usually means your most elderly relative. But then the relatives may also have a treasure trove of pictures you have never seen, and neither has anyone else.

I usually store my pictures on an external drive since these are things you never want to lose and should prize over all else. It is easy for picture to be lost as family members pass and quite often they are lost to the rest of the family. I tend to be the type of person who will ask if there are any pictures they are willing to loan me and this sometimes works. If not, I look to Ancestry and Facebook to fill in the gaps. I store all of the pictures as well as create hard copies of the photographs on photo paper. My walls are papered with dead people faces.

Since many of the pictures you will borrow to scan, keep track of who you are borrowing them from. I use envelopes and also make a list of the pictures I am borrowing and then match it up with those I am returning. Giving back the wrong pictures to the right person can create a genealogical Armageddon. Yes, there can be a full-out war when it comes to pictures—one that can last for generations—and as people pass away and are added to folders.

When I came across damaged pictures, I was always afraid the entire set of pictures would disintegrate in to dust. I decided to teach myself how to repair then. The first four pictures are tintypes. I borrowed them from and aunt who was in her 90s and she allowed me to scan them. They were in very poor condition, but after about 60 hours each, I was able to repair them.

You will need a graphics software package. I use of Picture Publisher V. 8. It retails for less than $20 and the learning curve is very easy. You can purchase more expensive software, but I have found the more expensive the software the more difficult to learn.

When I am repairing a tintype, I use small bit of alike background and copy and paste it over the damaged areas—I mean very small—no more than a few pixels.

The first picture took 40 incremental repairs and the second about 20. But I feel the work was well worth is since now we have a clean picture of teenage relatives, which are often less obtainable.

The third picture is from a post card that was damaged. Again, I used very small sections of similar background to copy and paste over the damage. You sometimes need to use a very fine smear tool to blend the repairs with the new and old repaired material.

I am currently working on older photographs that have been damaged. I want to make sure everyone can make out the image and recognize their dead relatives. Creating a new eye is one of the most difficult task, as is anything having to do with the face. It is the slowest process and people relative are always anxious to see your work, but people need to be able to recognize the family member so you need to be care not to repair things too quickly.

EXAMPLES OF REPAIRED PICTURES

REPAIRED TINTYPES

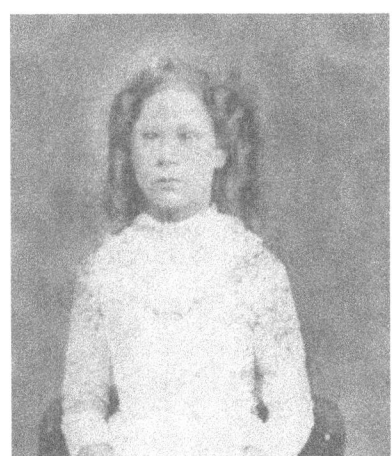

REPAIRED POSTCARD

GHOSTS
Chapter 9

Death certificates, writings on headstones, cemeteries newspapers. These are my first love. I enjoy nothing more than to wander though cemeteries reading the headstones. There are so many stories carved on headstones—stories you rarely see anymore. At a cemetery in south east Oregon that was struck hard during the WWI, you rarely saw a soldier's grave. You instead saw headstone after headstone pertaining to the Spanish Influenza—mothers, soldiers, fathers and children all laid side by side all having had died within days of one another. This is the kind of history you find in cemeteries where everyone is a ghost.

I have found that all, or at least most, ghost stories have some strand of truth, even though it may have been embellished somewhat as the story unfolded and was passed from generation to generation.

During my grandmother's younger years she lived with her grandparents. She remembers that her step-uncle was brought back by ship and then rode the train home from the war front after passing away from Spanish Influenza. When the body of Robert arrived, the story says his frantic mother opened the coffin to give her son one

41

last kiss. That kiss was said to have spread Spanish Influenza. Through the eyes of a six-year-old, the influenza became the Black plague. And it wasn't just through my grandmother's eyes. Throughout the county, word spread that it was the Bubonic Plague that killed Uncle Robert and many others in the small communities. The six-year-old was surrounded by death. More

than half the town fell to influenza, including my great grandfather and his wife—Grandpa Robert died two before his wife Anna.

Another story that appears to have been somewhat true was the tale of Grace Lillian. When Grace was about twelve-years-old, she fell ill and died. She was buried in the town cemetery and nothing more was thought of her after a year or so of flower laying by her mother.

The town where Grace Lillian was buried was constantly flooding so they moved the entire town five miles north, including

the cemetery. When they dug up Grace Lillian's grave the lid came off the old wooden coffin and they found that Grace Lillian had been buried alive. According to the doctor, Grace Lillian must have fallen

into such a deep sleep that she was thought to be dead.

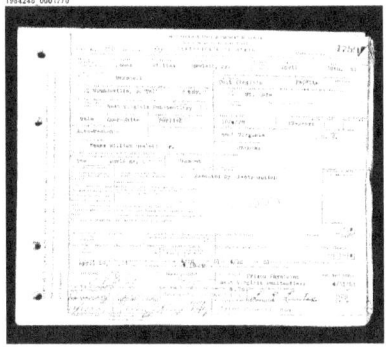

Later, when my mother and I traveled to the area, we did find the cemetery where Grace Lillian was laid to rest. She had a tiny headstone with a carved lamb. We placed a small bunch of flowers on the headstone wondering if the story were true.

My grandmother believed it to be true and she and other family members insisted on EKGs before they were laid to rest. My grandmother wasn't born when Grace Lillian passed away, but she knew the story well enough to be able to recite it on cold winter nights.

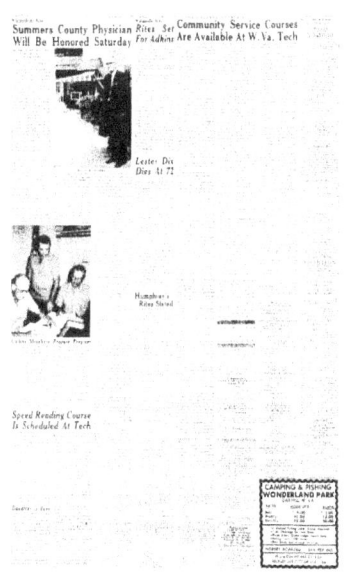

Another story that kept us up all night was true. A great cousin of mine was a murderer. I didn't know him. He was on my father's side of the family and they knew very little of each other. Apparently, after being turned down by the military twice in one month, he got drunk and caught a cab into town. Once there, he beat the cab driver to death. He later confessed to the crime.

My cousin was considered mentally deficient (moron was the

term then), but this made no difference to the court. After a brief trial, he was convicted. During that time, and prior to his being put to death, he was treated like royalty. He was offered cigarettes by the chief of police and he had his picture taken with innumerable people who wanted to document their time spent with a killer.

Had the story not been so gruesome, it would almost be pitiful. No tears were shed, and my cousin was convinced he was some sort of newspaper celebrity. In fact, they reported on everything from the clothes he wore to the type of cigarettes he smoked. His last meal drew a thousand or more readers.

When my cousin finally received his punishment in April 1955, it had been only two months since the actual murder. He entered the room where he was to be put to death with a smile and he shook hands with the crowd. My cousin was the last person put to death by 'Old Sparky'. This was prior to the criminal justice system moving to the gas chamber. Either way, for awhile my cousin was a star. James is said to roam the halls of the prison in the room where Old Sparky is kept.

There is also the story of a young mother who traveled from Scotland alone at the age of 16 and later died giving birth to her son, my great great grandfather. Of course, the story is embellished with bits and pieces no one could really could have known, but through my genealogy search, I have found the core of the story to be true. Mary Hanna, from Scotland, did come to America on her own and did die in childbirth. This is now well-documented. It is said that Mary wanders through the cemetery in Peoria where her child was lain wailing for her baby.

In another story my Great Aunt Mary died in an asylum after being beaten so bad by her husband that she had a 'damaged brain'. Again the story is embellished, but basically true. Mary is said to haunt the asylum searching for her husband seeking revenge.

My great great grandfather was born on a ship while crossing the Atlantic. Trying to find him was almost impossible until I found a story from his son. Of course there are lots of storms and creaking and such, but the story is true. His mother was said to have died on the ship and Cornelius went to his grave wailing for his mother who had been tossed from the ship, her dead body floating on the icy waters.

I never fail to tell the tale to anyone if they ask me about Great Grandmother Susie's hidden will or the story that her husband poisoned her. Yet there are those times I just sit quietly in the corner and let the ghosts come out to play through other voices. Susie is said to send messages to the living in an attempt to let them know where the will is hidden and about the poisoning. Again, come kernel of truth.

My grandmother used to love to tell us the story of an old man in a rocking chair, rocking away in the attic. We could only hear it at night and only while sleeping in the living room in the front of the gas heater. Grandma also decided that one bedroom was haunted. No one under the age of 27 would sleep in that room so we were all stuck with the old man in the attic.

No matter if your dead people are recent or centuries past, there will always be a story. For the newly dead, it make take a century for the tale to be told And then again, it may only take a decade or two. The stories change though time and then solidify into a nighttime ghoul–fest. I have often wondered what my haunted tale will be--most likely that my best friends were dead people.

CREATING KEEPSAKES
Chapter 10

Before you begin making a keepsake, first have a plan. You will to get together all that you will need for your project. If you are using pictures and documents, make sure you have stored them for easy access, something we will talk about later.

I have made keepsakes using a variety of online and offline methods. I haven't always had the best of luck using some online programs, but there are a few. I really do like the ability to create online It give other family members the opportunity to see your work and to possibly purchase it.

I have had better luck using old school software like Microsoft Publisher. I am able to choose backgrounds, insert photos and clipart, and arrange the project how I would like as well as decide how many pages I would like to include. Once I finish the project, I upload it to Amazon's Create Space. There are examples of how the book needs to be formatted, which is pretty much set up the margins so the book prints correctly. I have made a family album, a recipe book, and a book for my immediate family. Once the books have been made and uploaded to Amazon, family members can go to the website and order them just like any other book for a minimal price, which is another thing I like when I compare the work to MyCanvas. I do like MyCanvas charts better.

Other keepsakes include T-shirts and maps. T-shirts are an inexpensive way to allow reunion attendees to take something home with them. Be creative. When my family went on a tour of south eastern Oregon, the T-shirts read "Reunion 2006" on the front and "Alvord Desert Tour" on the back. I always recommend that you get a list of who plans to buy one and maybe even collect the money up front. I would also suggest they be professionally printed. They fade less and are a memento that can last far into the future and carry with it a great deal of memories. Oftentimes family members have signed each other's shirts complete with addresses and phone numbers.

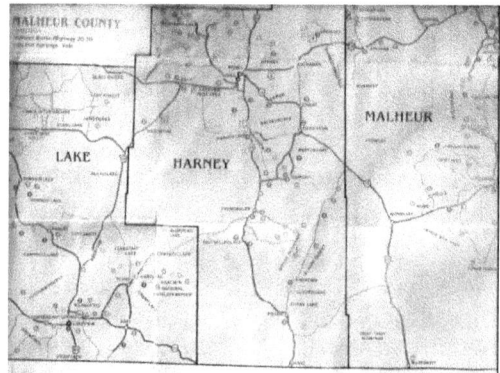 Another keepsake is a map of the tour, printed, and including all of the sites the group will be seeing along the way. We have combined our own map with those from the Forest Service and created a binder with a clear cover for the tour map. Inside is a map of things to see and places to go and pictures of ruins and extra paper for taking

notes,

With a little creativity and a lot of patience you can produce any number and types of keepsakes. Copied of bibles with genealogy information written in them can be a special gift. There are also premade books you can buy to fill in family information as a group during a family get-together.

I have taken stacks of paper I have collected and copied and bound them with twine and a cover to give as a gift. I also include photocopied pictures to include in the booklets.

CDs also make wonderful keepsakes for a reunion (although I have known to pass them out at funerals), Make sure each photograph or document on the CD is labeled, For instance, a picture of Aunt Cora may just say b:\aaokarka. No

one but the original writer will be able to decipher this. Rename files so they make sense. Using the same file, you can rename it Ann Spear from Arkansas. This was everyone know who is in the picture and where they are from and how they may have lived. When you rename a file just right click on it while it is in the folder and then follow the directions.

Once you have named the file, anyone you pass on the pictures or documents to will always know who or what they are looking at. Since most files downloaded use a series of numbers and letters, it

is easier to name them as you download them. This will be useful when you add them to your keepsake.

However you choose to create your keepsakes, make them meaningful and make them something that can be passed down for generations. Not everyone in the family is going to interested in dead people and all the work it takes to gather their life stories, but there will be a few, and as my grandmother used to call them, "The Keepers of the Flame".

ACCESSING ANCESTRY
Chapter 13

I started my genealogy quest when Ancestry was still free. It is now $19.95 for a US membership and $29.95 for a Global membership (although these prices may have changed). Ancestry is probably the best place to start. There are others who have  searched the same ancestors as you will be searching and they may have pictures and stories as well as dates and birthplaces. Just be careful. I only use Ancestry Member Trees as a starting point if I can't find documentation. Not every time, but sometimes, the information is incorrect and people just copy the incorrect information over and over again—and at the speed of light. I may initially use the compiled information, but I always keep track. Much of the time, I just ignore it.

I like the middle name aspect of Ancestry. You are often able to prove or disprove information based on middle names. It is a tradition, in many cases, for the mother's maiden name to be the middle name of a male child, or a female child for that matter. I have found and confirmed a number of relatives this way, So always look at middle names and middle initials—it may lead you in the right direction.

If you are obsessive, like I am, you will never be able to ignore the little leaf that indicates a hint. A hint is possible information on someone you are researching or have already researched. This is how you end up with 22,860 people in your tree. But then again, remember, dead people can be your best friends. Especially when you find out their secrets. They like to whisper in your ear and that is what keeps you running after

them—you want to hear what they have to say.

The first voices I heard were my own. I put all of all I had collected into my tree before I started my searches. I

wanted to make sure I had the truth entered for my relatives. I included pictures of aunts and uncles and second cousins (all dead, of course). People argued with me even though I knew the dead relative quite well; however, they had found contradictory information on Ancestry. Next thing I knew, my late aunt became a picture of my great grandmother and had lived and died at least 50 years in the past. I felt compelled to argue, but did so in a tiny voice and let it drop. I knew my dead aunt and as long as I had her information correct, she would care less that someone she didn't know had it wrong.

Ancestry has other issues, too. Often times, you can search and find nothing on the person you are looking for; then as you look for a dead relative of the dead relative, the first dead relative pops up. Frustrating because it can sometimes be hard to find your way back to the first dead relative. I find myself keeping a legal pad next to my laptop for dead relative hints of my own. The pads fill up quickly, but sometimes it is the only way to keep track.

Once you add information about one of your ancestors in

 Ancestry, you will find that within seconds, someone else has entered the same information. This isn't because they found the same information as you have—it's just that it gets added to the member pages and with millions of people searching at once, it's quite possible they are swooping in to grab your information. This is where the problem lies—your information becomes your hint and this can go on forever with both hints, pictures and stories. It is a never-ending cycle.

Getting lost is also a hazard of using Ancestry. How do you keep track of everyone in your tree and make sure your information is correct. After I have twenty or so new people, I go back and check all of the documentation and then add a star in the space for a suffix to show the information had been confirmed. For the suffix, I just add a space and put it in the box with the last name. That shows me I have verified the dead person's information and that they belong on a branch of my tree.

Probably the most difficult thing to deal with in Ancestry is that little mailbox. Sometimes you meet a wonderful new addition to your family—most often the second cousin of you uncle's stepfathers mother-in-law. It is still a wonderful discovery, however. Then there are those who continue to send you mail even though you have

explained to them a zillion times that your mother was not married to a man named Jacob and she did not live and die in the 1800s. Her picture is not a tintype and you are not 164 years old. See what I am getting at here.

You might also find duplicates of just about everything— duplicate photos, duplicate wills, scenery, headstones, group photos and sometimes your face (but the face you are wearing is not your own). I add the duplicates and kill them later so I don't lose the information. It's an arduous process, but one you will appreciate later.

Another difficulty with Ancestry is that you can get so far ahead of yourself that you never have the chance to go back and look at all the photographs, census records, wills and bible entries or read all the stories you've collected. As you are adding people and their information, you just add and keep adding and forget to look back. As soon as I finish my tree, which I may be a part of by then, I would like to go back and look at the histories. However, I currently have 4,841 photos, 16,659 records and 1,031 stories. If I finish within the next two years, I might have a chance to at least get started. However, I have now begun my DNA search so the discovery is most likely to continue.

STORING YOUR INFORMATION
Chapter 14

One of the worst things that can happen is if you lose electronic or hardcopy data. I store my data in several ways. I scan

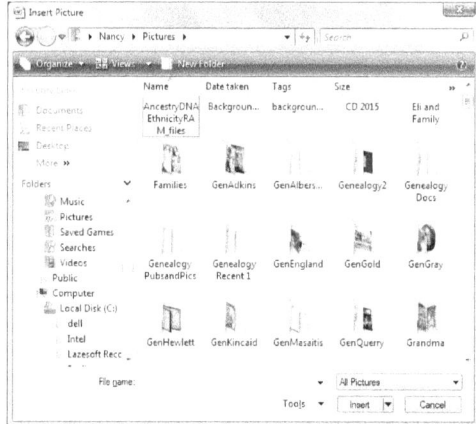

all of my hardcopies and save them to folders that I have created with the name of the branch of the tree. Then I organize the hardcopies by the tree as well. Once this is done, I save everything to a CD, a

thumb drive and backup computer.

Some things are sent to you via email and you have no hardcopy so I print one to go into my files, as well as make sure there are back-ups. When you have been collecting for a long time, like I have, it is easy to lose things in the shuffle if you are not careful.

Also, as I said previously remember to label things appropriately. I have had

pictures emailed to me that are labeled 'c:\pfhenakktex' and I have no idea what that means. Luckily the sender will say, 'This is Aunt Phyllis Henry from Texas'. I label all copies 'Phyllis Henry from Texas' add dates and any other information I may have and put them in the appropriate folder—hard copies and electronic copies.

I also print up any emails anyone sends about my family's history. I scan them as well and the print hard copies. If I get stuck at some point, I can always go back and read the email.

CHECK YOUR WORK
Chapter 15

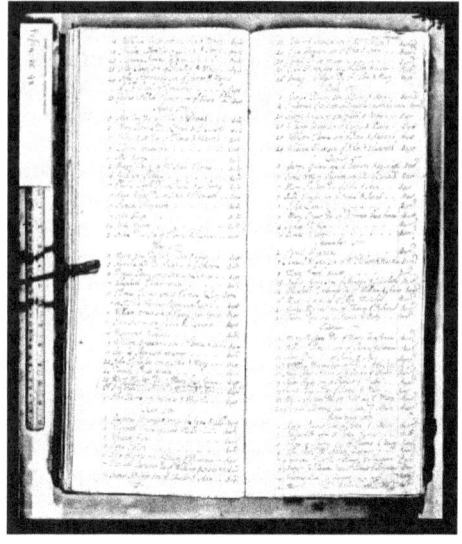

Whether you are using Ancestry or Rootsweb, remember, most data was entered by people just like you and me and there will be errors. Always check your work and the work of others. Even if it sometimes takes a little more research.

As I said in the chapter about Ancestry and errors, you may find a 300-hundred year old relative born in 1967 in Alameda, California. People perpetrate this error by just copying the data to their own tree. Always check to see if what you are adding to your tree makes sense.

It may take more research to find out what the truth is about your dead person. I look for additional correct documentation. If there is no correct documentation, then I strike them from my tree. It may be hard to let go, but remember, that one error can be copied into millions of other trees if someone decides not to check their work.

Census records are a great way to find the truth about your relative. I use census records all of the time to verify my data. I look for family members I know are part of the group and I look at age and where they live and what their occupation is at the time the census record was recorded. If you know that your great great grandfather had seven children and a wife named Mary and a birthday of 1822, you probably have the right person. However, I also look at wills, church records and other documents. I don't allow my dead people to slip past without at least some documentation. That doesn't mean you can't believe everything you see, it just means that you need to make sure everything you

see is believable.

Other things you need to check are parents and wives. Someone may have had three wives with children from each wife, but their parents will always be the same. Again, you will need to do your research. Finding parents can be easier than you might think if you look at marriage and church records. Wherever it is that you look, be sure the wife and children you chose are the ones that are yours. Just adding the one listed at the top, doesn't mean that this is your relative. It could be that your dead people are farther down the list. Again, be sure to check your work.

You might also find children who were given over as wards to other family members, especially in poorer communities. Children were also placed in orphanages. If you can't find a child in the census or if you find the child listed as a ward or as adopted, it is going to be harder to find the child's parents.

Census records are a great way to find a child if the child's parents were living at the last census. Marriage records also hold a wealth of information.

For example, one of my dead people was placed in an orphanage/poor house in the early 1800s. I found a previous census record that held the information I needed to get started, There were other children in the same orphanage with the same names as the other children. From

this, I could surmise the parents were deceased. I then also had the parents' names. By checking marriage, newspapers, archives and death records. I found that the parents had died in a flood.

With this information, I was able to follow the children to see if they were adopted or if they remained orphans. I found that boys left the orphanages alone, often times at the ages of 14 – 16. These boys were then listed as farmhands. With this research, I was able to track down my relative and complete the line.

In another confusing instance, I found a grandfather with three different last names. I knew the last name I was given, but the information wasn't correct. I combed through marriage records and found that my grandfather's mother had been married several times. Each time she remarried, my grandfather took the last name of the new husband. When my great grandmother married the last time, my grandfather remained with his stepfather and permanently took his last name.

I found the correct last name and had traced back my

grandfather, but then I began looking for his brothers and sisters. Again I relied on census records and death records. Death records most often show the parents of the person who died and I was able to match up the parents with the brothers and sisters of my grandfather, as well as their spouses.

I continued to grow my tree by following this line until I realized there was no real purpose to finding great aunt's spouse's cousin's mother, so I stopped when the line began to explode as did other lines.

During the numerous explosions, I realized I had duplicates. I had to go back and determine which was the correct dead person and which on was just a placeholder, This was, and still is, tiring, but again, you want your information to be correct. I didn't use place holders often, but I did use them. I would add a name to my tree until I found the corrected name with researched information. This meant I had to go back and purge, but it is well worth the time considering how it would damage the validity of your tree as well as the trees of others.

Stories, oral histories, documents, newspapers, church records and other archived information will help you keep your information as clean and clear as possible. Not to say that we don't all make mistakes. But using documentation and research, you can find what is real and what is a figment of Grandma's imagination.

KNOWING WHEN TO QUIT
Chapter 16

Every time you add someone to your tree, you will undoubtedly add another 60—it's just math. Most families had 8, 9, or even 13 or 14 children—so you add the children, their children, and pretty soon you have just added 600 people who are all having children.

At one point I had about 15 or 20 people in my tree. Just parents, grandparents, and great grandparents. Then they all started to look interesting, and now, after 25 years of searching, I have 16, 661 (after today's count) and I know each and every one of them to some extent—and a lot of the times I wish I didn't. At one point I was up to 22,000, but I began weeding and trimming. Most were duplicates (how could that happen) and others led nowhere—no connection. Oddly enough, it was a good feeling to delete here and there and think 'no more little leaves for that one.'

The ones that do stay are significant or insignificant, depending on how you look at it. I would say about two-thirds of mine are insignificant as in I don't really care about who they are and who their children or parents might be But if you find yourself caring about one of your dead people, you will find yourself caring about their children as well—their children, their great grandchildren, their great-great grandchildren...

You also need to think about how far back you want to go, I have a documented line back to the Crusades. The next generations married and begat and married and begat and continued doing so for branch upon branch. But it was fascinating and I ended up paying for ancestry's global subscription just to dig for more. Digging the roots makes taller the tree.

You might also stumble onto someone that you suddenly have an attachment to—like someone who was a widow at a young age and lost all of her children except for one to the black plague. And yes, it is possible to find that information. They are the 10th great grandfather of your cousins uncle's mother-in-law, but that's okay—someone has to let her out of her box (or coffin, whatever you prefer).

Then there are the people who bring you new people—people you never knew existed. And who can resist a new face. Could it be the missing link you have been searching for—or maybe a whole new branch (God forbid). Whoever it is, if you are obsessed, like I am, you will add them to your tree and start searching—head down, fingers flying, oohs and ahhhs every time you find a new fact or an image.

I am definitely a user. It's rather unnerving, but I add people to my tree the minute I know they are dead—this way I won't forget. As soon as someone is dead, their begets are added and we are off to plant a branch one again. Pruning comes later. Most people don't have a problem with it. I attach pictures, obituaries, etc. as if I were reporting the death in a newspaper. There is even a place for comments. I do every once in awhile have someone say, 'Their body isn't even cold yet'. They don't understand that I consider myself 'the keeper of the flame', the person who makes sure that family members live forever in a way—that is what I tell myself anyway.

You will need to decide for yourself when it's enough—when to snuff out your flame. Nearly 25 years later, I still have boxes and an ottoman full of papers and I continue to collect. I now have my laptop conveniently sitting on a tray in front of the TV with the internet endlessly open to Ancestry and other sites. Some days I feel like a sadist—especially when I have to copy one more image of a 300 year old headstone that is pretty much unreadable. But I most likely will never stop. I won't ever know when to quit. Sometimes I think there should be a club for those of us who are obsessed with ghosts—some place where we can each stand up and say, *"Hi, my name is _____, and I am addicted to dead people.*

Notes

_____

_____

_____

_____

_____

_____

_____

_____

_____

_____

_____

_____

_____

_____

_____

_____

_____

_____

_____

_____

GETTING STARTED ON YOUR TREE

□ Use the note section write down a list of where you have gathered information and what you have gathered.

□ Collect your information from all of the sources I have mentioned, including living relatives, libraries, museums and on-line sources.

□ Check you work and if you use another person's work, check it as well.

□ Use the example to start laying out your tree. The lower branches will include your most resent relatives. You will then work your way to the top of the tree as you find more and more relatives who have passed on.

□ Store your work! Use the hard drive of your computer and an external drive of some kind like a CD or a thumb drive.

□ Scan hardcopies and store them in two places as well.

□ Organize your computer files so you can find things when you need them.

□ Organize your computer genealogy files.

www.ingramcontent.com/pod-product-compliance
Lightning Source LLC
Chambersburg PA
CBHW070319290526
45791CB00003B/1178